The Art of HODLING

A Beginner's Guide to Cryptocurrency Trading and Investing

Martin Quest

© Copyright 2018 - All rights reserved.

This document is geared towards providing exact and reliable information in regard to the topic and issue covered. The publication is sold on the idea that the publisher is not required to render an accounting, officially permitted, or otherwise, qualified services. If advice is necessary, legal or professional, a practiced individual in the profession should be ordered.

- From a Declaration of Principles which was accepted and approved equally by a Committee of the American Bar Association and a Committee of Publishers and Associations.

In no way is it legal to reproduce, duplicate, or transmit any part of this document by either electronic means or in printed format. Recording of this publication is strictly prohibited and any storage of this document is not allowed unless with written permission from the publisher. All rights reserved.

The information provided herein is stated to be truthful and consistent, in that any liability, in terms of inattention or otherwise, by any usage or abuse of any policies, processes, or directions contained within is the solitary and utter responsibility of the recipient reader. Under no circumstances will any legal responsibility or blame be held against the publisher for any reparation, damages, or monetary loss due to the information herein, either directly or indirectly.

Respective authors own all copyrights not held by the publisher.

The information herein is offered for informational purposes solely and is universal as so. The presentation of the information is without a contract or any type of guarantee assurance.

The trademarks that are used are without any consent, and the publication of the trademark is without permission or backing by the trademark owner. All trademarks and brands within this book are for clarifying purposes only and are the owned by the owners themselves, not affiliated with this document.

Table of Contents

Introduction

Chapter 1: What is Money?

Chapter 2: Why Cryptocurrencies Work

Chapter 3: How To Store Your Bitcoins Or Altcoins Safely

Chapter 4: Is Bitcoin dead? -

Chapter 5: Cryptocurrency Pre-Hodling Strategies

Chapter 6: Cryptocurrency Hodling Strategies

Conclusion

Introduction

Cryptocurrencies have become all the rage over the last few months, especially after the meteoric rise in the price of Bitcoin back in December 2017. It used to be that cryptocurrency investing was the realm of experts and savvy investors. But because of Bitcoin's massive success and popularity after December 2017, things have changed. It has now expanded to include even the smallest and least experienced of investors. Before going into the details of hodling and cryptocurrencies in general, it would be very beneficial for you to get a glimpse of how cryptocurrencies became what they are now.

Brief History of Cryptocurrencies

It all began in the 1990s when American cryptographer, David Chaum, created what was considered as the first kind of online money in the Netherlands: DigiCash. He created DigiCash as an extension of an encryption algorithm that was considered popular during those times, which was RSA. The technology he created, together with its eCash product, was able to generate a huge amount of attention from the media. It became so popular that Microsoft Corporation tried to buy DigiCash for $180 million with the intention of placing DigiCash on every computer in the world that ran on the Windows operating system. One of the crucial mistakes Chaum and his company made was to reject Microsoft's $180 million offer and earn the ire of De Nederlandsche Bank (Netherland's Central Bank), which was the Netherland's primary monetary authority. All of those crucial mistakes eventually led to the demise of DigiCash in 1998, when the company went bankrupt.

The second generation of Internet money was borne from the learning experiences of DigiCash. Companies from this generation came up with alternative payment solutions and money systems that were also Internet-based but with small but important changes. Of these companies, the clear winner was PayPal. The reason why PayPal trumped its competition was its ability to give users what they really wanted in the first place, which was money on the web browser platforms they were already familiar with. PayPal - unlike its peers back in the day - was able to give its users the ability to transfer money to and from merchants and buyers, respectively, using a seamless peer-to-peer money transfer system. PayPal's massive success is very obvious by the fact that next only to credit cards, it's the most popular means by which to transact online.

But wait - there's more! PayPal's success led to other companies emulating it. One of the systems that tried to walk on the same path as PayPal was e-Gold. Unlike PayPal, its primary currency was gold, i.e., it received physical gold as deposits from its users and in return, it issued e-Gold or gold credits. E-Gold was able to manage a relatively healthy amount of cross-border transactions using gold. But because of the prevalence of fraudulent investment scams like Ponzi schemes, e-Gold was closed.

The next significant event in the history of cryptocurrencies is the 2008 subprime mortgage crisis that nearly crippled the financial system of the United States and affected many of the world's major financial institutions. This event served as some kind of wakeup call to many of the world's major economies and has led to the emergence of what is now popularly known as the blockchain, which is the foundation of cryptocurrencies today as we know them.

In 2009, an anonymous person (or group) that went by the identity of Satoshi Nakamoto published a white paper that expounded, among other things, the source code, technology and concept of what is now called the blockchain. And together with the blockchain, he launched the granddaddy of all cryptocurrencies as we know it; Bitcoin. The blockchain, while not an earthshattering, disruptive or incremental technology, was considered a foundational one. Why foundational? It's because it was meant to - and it still does - serve as a bedrock upon other data network storage technologies can be built. The blockchain naturally challenges all the conventional online data management protocols of that time, which included centralization of data.

Today, there are more than 16 million units of Bitcoin that are circulating in the digital financial system and these have a total market capitalization of around $50 billion. More importantly, Bitcoin's already garnering increasing acceptance and support from both the I.T. and business communities alike. As part of its gradual integration into the financial mainstream, some economic powerhouse countries like Australia, Canada and Japan have already begun regulating Bitcoins through tax and legal measures.

Since 2009, the growth in the popularity of the blockchain and Bitcoins has surged. This surge in popularity gave birth to other cryptocurrencies, which are referred to as altcoins or alternative coins to Bitcoin. Today, there are more than 850 cryptocurrencies in the digital financial system being transacted internationally, which include Ethereum (Ether), Ripple, Litecoin, Monero and Stratis. And if you combine the total market capitalization of all altcoins with that of Bitcoin, the result would exceed $100 billion.

Because of the massive expansion of cryptocurrencies, it appears that cryptocurrencies have created an entirely new and global industry. Because of the massive advances in the blockchain technology, as evidenced by the growth in the number of cryptocurrencies on the market today, newly developed apps that will be created upon the blockchain technology will naturally use cryptocurrencies. And as more and more cryptocurrency platforms and exchanges start to emerge, more and more people will be able to use blockchain-based apps, which in turn will make the latter industry grow even more.

Ethereum

When talking about the history of cryptocurrencies, a discussion of the second biggest and most established cryptocurrency - Ethereum - can't be ignored. Ether - as it's more commonly referred to - is an open source blockchain platform that features among others, a collection of programming languages upon which other blockchain apps can be built (Decentralized Apps), the Ethereum Virtual Machine, and smart contracts.

Ether's a relatively young altcoin compared to most other major ones, having been created only in late 2013, by a dude named Vitalik Buterin and publicly launched in July 2015. But considering its relatively young age, Ether has been able to garner unmatched support from the business, consumer and developer communities because of the massive promise it has shown. Its market capitalization has already exceeded $30 billion and because of its open source nature, Ether has made it possible for a lot of startup companies to create their own cryptocurrencies on its platform. And Ether's popularity is expected to increase even more because of its trademark Enterprise Ethereum Alliance (a group of international and cutting-edge businesses that both use and assist the Ethereum platform), its technological advantage over all other blockchain platforms, its relatively huge developer community, and its relatively easy development.

The Future of Cryptocurrencies

One of the main motivations that fuel the development of cryptocurrencies is the breaking down of existing financial and technological barriers and borders, particularly in the realm of trade and finance. More than 1,000 altcoins are vying with each other in terms of early blockchain developmental stages. As a result, we can reasonably expect to see only a couple of successful cryptocurrencies to stay and change the way we will pay, lend money, borrow money, trade, and do banking in the future. And in the near future, we can reasonably expect several major cryptocurrencies to be accepted in the financial mainstream, which can signal a whole new era of digital finance.

HODLing

The main topic of this book is hodling. But what does hodl mean? The first instance when this term was used was in 2013 at the Bitcoin talk forum. One of its members with the handle GameKyuubi used the term hodl under a thread named "I Am Hodling." It appears from the post that while trying to convey his conviction of holding on to his Bitcoins despite how its prices nosedived at that time, he was drunk. As a result, he seems to have misspelled the world "hold" as "hodl." And it seems to have caught on with a lot of people because the word has become very popular in the cryptocurrency industry to the point that many cryptocurrency traders/investors use it to communicate the idea that they're holding on to their cryptocurrencies regardless of what happens. And what was once considered a typographical error has since evolved into a funny acronym: Holding On for Dear Life.

How to Use This Guide

This book is meant to help or guide you to increase your chances of successfully hodling cryptocurrencies, i.e., making good money out of them. After all, there's only one reason or motivation for holding on to financial assets, and that's to earn significant returns from them. Otherwise, what's the point?

This book is divided into 5 parts; a discussion on the nature of money or fiat currencies, what makes cryptocurrencies work and worth investing in, general principles for safely holding your Bitcoins or other cryptocurrencies, why Bitcoin is here to stay and how to invest in or hodl cryptocurrencies. By the end of the book, you'll be in a very good position to start hodling cryptocurrencies. But the best way to use this guide is to act on the information it gives. Without application, everything you'll learn here is just trivia. This book's value, as well as that of any other non-fiction or self-help book, is in the application of knowledge. So after finishing this book, I strongly encourage you to act on what you've learned.

Chapter 1: What is Money?

To better understand or appreciate cryptocurrencies, it's important to get a good grasp of the nature of money. This is because cryptocurrencies are a form of money and by understanding the true nature of money, especially what important characteristics it should possess, you'll be able to better appreciate and understand the nature of cryptocurrencies. And in turn, you'll be able to better understand the principle of hodling.

What is Money?

At its very core, money is something that is used to represent the value of other things. For example, you gave me money in exchange for receiving a copy of this book, and that sum of money represents the value of this book. The money I received from you and others who have bought this book, I'll use to purchase or acquire something of value from other vendors today or tomorrow. If you study history, you'll see that the values of things have been expressed in different forms and money, the primary way by which values have been expressed has come in different shapes and materials. Case in point, things like gold, shells, wheat and salt have been used in the past to represent value and as a medium of exchange. But for something to be able to continue representing value, the people who are using it must continue trusting that a medium of exchange is indeed valuable and more importantly, its value will persist for a long time so that they will still be able to benefit from it in the future.

How People's Trust in Money Has Evolved

Only until one or two centuries ago, societies had always placed their trust in something when it comes to the value or representation of money. But the way people trust in money has shifted from trusting something to trusting someone. What do I mean by this?

In the past, people would use - as I mentioned earlier - stuff like gold, wheat, salt and even seashells as a medium of exchange or money. But over time, people caught on to the fact that using such things as a measure of value and medium of exchange can be quite burdensome. Can you imagine buying your groceries with seashells or salt? What if inflation was very high the last several years and you want to buy a month's worth of groceries? Can you imagine bringing that much salt to the supermarket? And if you're the grocery owner, can you imagine having to weigh the salt being paid to you by your customers and needing a very large space and vehicle to store and transport all that salt? And what if it rains? Do you get the picture?

Because of such inconvenience, people were forced to improvise and come up with a more practical value storage and payment solution; paper money! So this was how it worked in the beginning. When you take up a bank or the government's offer to take physical possession of your gold bars for storage, they'd issue you certificates or bills for the amount or value of the gold you deposited with them. Say your gold bars were worth $500, the bank or the government taking possession of your gold bars would issue you a paper certificate or bills worth $500.

Now think about this. Which is easier to carry around - paper bills worth $500 or gold worth $500? Another thing to think about is this. Which is easier to cut in smaller pieces or value, paper bills or a gold bar? If you want to buy a bag of chips for $5, you'd only have to give the cashier five $1 bills, but if you're carrying around $500 worth of gold, you'd have to cut it proportionately to an amount that closely or exactly represents $5.

Another thing worth thinking about back in the day is this. If you wanted your gold bars back, all you'd need to do is give $500 worth of bills or certificates back to the bank or government to redeem your gold bars. It's that simple. Because of the convenience and practicality it brings, paper money has grown so much in popularity and has become the primary means by which goods and services are bought and sold all over the world today.

Back in the day, the value of the United States dollar was linked or based on gold. The money of the United States of America was valued based on its gold holdings. This was referred to as the Gold Standard. But over time, the macro economy has changed and as a result, the link connecting the value of the United States dollar to the value of gold was cut. As a result, Americans - and the rest of the world, considering the US$ has become the world's primary currency - had been conditioned to shift their trust from gold to the Federal government. In other words, people have been conditioned to shift their trust when it comes to monetary value from something - gold - to someone who assumed responsibility for the value of the dollar, which is the Federal government. And the only reason this system continues to work is trust because let's face it, there's no real underlying asset of worth behind the value of the dollar or other currencies. This was how fiat or paper money was born.

Fiat Money

The word "fiat" is a Latin word that's best interpreted as "by decree." This means that any fiat currency, i.e., paper money, only has value because their respective governments say so. As a result of such legal decrees of value, paper or fiat currencies are also called "legal tender" which means they have to be accepted for payment of goods and services in their respective countries. That being said, you can now see that money as we know it today has value only because of its legal status, which is declared by governments. As I mentioned earlier, the trust in the value of money has shifted from something (gold) to someone (the government).

Now fiat money as we know it now has some pretty serious issues. These are being centralized and are practically unlimited in quantity. Being centralized means that there's a central or lone authority that has the power to issue and control its supply, which in the case of the United States dollar is the Federal Reserve. It's also practically unlimited in quantity because the Federal Reserve has the power and capability to print or mint more units of the US dollar if it chooses to do so. Now, why is this a serious concern?

The reason is one of the most basic principles of economics; supply and demand. To be more specific, this means that when the supply of an object is increased, the value of that object will tend to decrease assuming demand for that thing remains constant. Conversely, when the supply of an item is decreased, assuming constant demand, the value will increase. So if the Federal Reserve or any monetary authority prints more money, it'll flood markets with more of that currency, which can make it worth less, i.e., buy less of goods and services. So when you see the prices of goods and services rising substantially over the long term, it's not necessarily because they became more expensive but because the value of the currency, e.g., the United States dollar, has dropped due to increased supply.

Digitizing Money

The establishment of fiat money has made it easy - even mandatory - to create digital ones. The advent of the Internet and establishment of monetary authorities that control and issue money have made the idea of digitizing money, i.e., making the most of digital or online currencies and letting such authorities keep tabs on who owns how much, a feasible and even necessary one. Proof of this is the evolution of alternative modes of payment to the point that they have become the main methods for transacting today.

For example, credit cards, fund transfers and PayPal have become standard forms of payment these days. And in the United States, in particular, paying in cash is looked upon as unconventional or even suspicious in some cases. The ramifications of this evolution are huge. One of them is the ever shrinking amount of physical money circulating in many of the world's biggest economies and financial systems. As mentioned earlier, it's highly unusual now to pay for stuff in cash in the United States, unless you're talking about mom-and-pop stores and other very small businesses.

Becoming exceedingly digitized, how does money in its digital form work? And a more specific concern with the digitalization of money is this. What systems are in place to prevent double-spending of money, i.e., what's to stop me from digitally reproducing my money so that I'd have so much more than what I actually have? You know, like creating duplicate copies of my favorite songs for listening on my different devices.

Most financial institutions today address this issue with centralization. What this means is there's only one party responsible for keeping records of financial transactions under a particular system, i.e., keeping track of who owns what and how much. Everyone who transacts under such systems has an account, which has a specific ledger under which all transactions and balances are recorded and maintained. Everyone - including you and me - trust the systems of financial institutions to keep accurate records of our balances and these institutions, in turn, trust their computer systems. In short, the solution of centralization of records is based on a ledger that's stored in one big-ass computer system or network. Prior to the creation of the blockchain, there have been many attempts to create alternative digital forms of payment that have failed because of one very important issue; preventing double-spending sans a central authority. That's why the centralized records keeping solution has persisted until this day - it generally works.

Challenges Posed By a Centralized Monetary System

Whenever we give someone or a group of people total authority over something, there will be serious challenges that will need to be addressed. When it comes to doing so over the monetary system, there are three specific challenges that need to be addressed and these are corruption, mismanagement, and control.

There's a saying that absolute power corrupts absolutely. Central banks or monetary authorities such as the Federal Reserve, who have the legal mandates to print money and create value in the process, practically have the ability to control how value is created and destroyed in their respective countries and in the case of the Federal Reserve, in the whole world. And such legal mandates are akin to unlimited or absolute financial power. A very good example of this is the fiasco at Wells Fargo where its employees were ordered to clandestinely open fictitious bank and credit card accounts in an attempt to puff up the company's revenues and consequently, its net profits, for several years. And compared to monetary authorities, Wells Fargo isn't even an authority.

Mismanagement is simply when a manager or a steward acts in a way that is not consistent with how his or her boss - the owner - wants him or her to act. Mismanagement - in the case of monetary authorities - can happen when governments act against the interest of the people they govern. A very good example of this is the way the United States monetary authorities allowed major financial institutions to issue credit-linked notes or financial derivatives with mortgages that have very high default risks, which corrupt credit ratings agencies have rated as "investment grade." This has resulted in the near collapse of the United States financial system, which the Federal Reserve rescued by acting against the interest of the public by using public money, which the public has objected to, to save the biggest financial institutions from collapsing in 2008.

Another issue of mismanagement is printing of new money without proper consideration of the deflationary effects of such an action. As mentioned earlier, printing more money floods the financial system with too much money, which in turn can cause a specific currency's value to plunge or drop (law of supply and demand, remember?). A very good case of this is the Venezuelan government, who mismanaged the country's financial system and official currency by printing too much money. The Venezuelan currency has become practically worthless to the point that people started to measure its value by weight instead of amount.

Lastly, a central monetary authority means surrendering all control over the people's money to the government. Because governments have the legal mandate to control the money supply, they also have the authority to control your money in ways that can prove to be very unfavorable or unjust to you, e.g., freezing your bank accounts and keeping you from accessing your money. Keeping physical cash on hand doesn't mean the government can't keep you from beneficially using your money. Governments can still keep you from using your money for your benefit simply by revoking its legal tender status so you won't be able to use it for transactions, such as what India did in the past.

Gold And Silver

Let's talk about gold and silver. Why? Because of its connection to money. To be more specific, gold and silver aren't just investments - they're money! You might say "No, money is the US dollar or the British Pound!" Sorry to burst your bubble but those are merely currencies, as is the case with all fiat currencies in the world. But currency is different from money. First, currency is just a legal tender status, the value of which isn't determined by the people but by governments. Second, legit money has important characteristics that make it so and the United States dollar doesn't have all of them and as such, money is more than just a medium of exchanging goods and services. Here are the seven characteristics of legit money:

1) Durability, which is the reason why wheat and salt are no longer used as money;
2) Divisibility, which is the reason why paintings and other pieces of art aren't used as money;
3) Convenience of use, which is why copper or lead isn't used as money;
4) Consistency in value, which is why real estate is hardly used - if ever - to pay for goods or services;
5) It must have intrinsic value or value as it is, which is why paper isn't really money;
6) It must be limited in available quantity, which is the reason for not using iron or rocks as money; and
7) And lastly, it should have a long track record of acceptability.

Upon close evaluation, you'll find that only gold and silver actually meet these characteristics. If you look at financial assets like stocks, bonds, or even real estate, they don't pass the consistency test because their prices tend to fluctuate. For others likes stocks, chances are that stocks of companies from 100 years ago - save for a few big and strong ones - have either deteriorated in value or are no longer worth anything because the companies whose ownerships such stocks represent no longer exist. The only items whose purchasing powers have not only been maintained but have also increased over the long-term are gold and silver. If only for this characteristic alone, gold and silver have kicked the butts of many currencies that have failed over the last 5,000 years. And if you factor in the fact that gold and silver are the only items that continue to have high value since the early days of all civilizations on Earth, you'll see why fiat currencies aren't really money.

Gold And Silver: Can Their Values Be Manipulated?

To answer this question, I'll focus the discussion more on gold. Gold price manipulation is defined as any intentional efforts to control the prices of this most precious metal. This supposedly happens in major financial markets when gold traders intentionally attempt to influence gold prices via certain financial instruments, particularly derivatives. These traders may have been able to successfully cause short-term deviations from the real values of gold, but over the long-term, it doesn't appear to be so.

The United States' Securities and Exchange Commission (SEC) defines manipulation in greater detail as any intentional act whose purpose is to trick investors by artificially affecting or controlling the market for a specific asset and includes activities like quote rigging, and voluminous trades or transactions that are meant to paint a deceptive impression of demand for a particular asset and sway market prices in their (traders') favor. And when speaking of gold price manipulation, there's one particular type of manipulation that is believed to be prevalent and that is price suppression, i.e., manipulating gold prices downward.

A really good question to ask then is this. Are the prices of gold - and consequently silver - manipulated? If you ask enough number of gold traders or investors, they'll tell you that it can be. Even more, they'll probably tell you that they are being systematically manipulated right this very moment. Are they right?

There are several iterations of this belief. One is that central bankers control the prices of precious metals. Another iteration of this belief is that greedy private commercial bankers are the ones manipulating gold prices downward through derivative instruments (short-selling and futures contracts) and high-volume trades meant to paint a scenario of low and decreasing demand for gold and silver. When you look at theories like these, they seem plausible at first glance because of instances where gold prices were controlled in the past, such as when certain governments fixed the prices of gold for decades or when the London Gold Pool suppressed its prices. Add to the fact that very rarely do financial institutions get penalized for gold price manipulation and you have a very prevalent belief that indeed, gold and silver prices can be manipulated.

But if you look at the long-term price histories of gold and silver, it becomes exceedingly clear that the answer to our question is no, prices of these precious metals can't be manipulated. Check out academic papers on the subject and you'll find that no compelling evidence for the case of price suppression or manipulation exists. In fact, you'll find very clear cyclical patterns if you check out the long-term price charts of these two precious metals.

From a long-term view, particularly of the 2000s, you'll probably start to wonder how the heck people believed that price suppression for these two precious metals existed. And when you think about crying wolf, you may start to wonder why manipulation is selective, i.e., manipulation is responsible when prices go down and when prices are going up, it's the market that's pushing it up. And while we can't disprove the belief that the world's biggest players attempt to manipulate prices, their effects - if any - are very short-lived because it's practically impossible to suppress the true market price of gold in the market. Those who want to suppress the price of gold and silver over the long-haul simply don't have enough financial resources to do so. And any attempts to do so will only backfire soon because any significant drops in the prices of gold and silver will only increase demand for it and consequently, lead to an increase in their prices.

Naked Short-Selling

Many investors and traders of these 2 precious metals tend to certain financial institutions, particularly bullion banks, of naked short-selling in order to put downward pressure on prices. But does naked short-selling mean? Short-selling means selling something you don't have. So if you talk about short-selling gold bullions, it means you're selling gold bullions you don't have yet.

Now, why would you sell something you don't have yet and get into a whole lot of trouble for it? After all, isn't selling something you don't have considered fraud? Well, not really. You may not have the gold bullions yet, but you can borrow other people's gold bullion to sell them. And when the price of gold bullions drops, you can buy the same amount of gold bullions you borrowed for short-selling and in the process, make money. This type of short-selling is called "covered" short-selling because you cover yourself by first borrowing enough gold bullions to sell.

Naked short-selling is uncovered short-selling, i.e., you sell the bullions you don't have even when you haven't borrowed any to sell yet. Naked short-selling also happens when you short-sell gold bullions without any guarantee from other people that you can borrow enough bullions for short-selling from them. Naked short-selling can put you or any trader who does it at high risk of not being able to deliver the gold bullions sold to the buyer. Thus, the potential impact of naked shorts can be very serious.

There are "rumors" or "urban legends" that accuse the Federal government of using bullion banks to execute tons of naked gold short sales on the Commodities Exchange on its behalf to suppress the price of gold, maintain the US dollar's value, and gives these bullion banks the opportunity to make huge money by repurchasing the bullions at lower prices. Sounds so evil and believable, right?

But think about this: if the number of naked short-sellers and there naked-short positions were that significant, the drop in prices of gold would be so huge that it would generate a reciprocal spike in demand for it. And the huge spike in demand would just wipe out the price drop because of the law of supply and demand.

Another thing to consider is the practicality of executing huge amounts of naked short sales just to suppress or manipulate the price of gold or silver. To execute this strategy effectively to drop the price of these 2 precious metals, naked short selling institutions would have to purchase a huge number of futures contracts just to cover their naked short positions. And as the futures contracts mature, they'd either have to buy the actual amounts of huge metals per futures contracts bought or rollover their positions, buy contracts that will be expiring, and flip the next ones out. In either case, the institutions involved in naked short-selling for price suppression will need to eventually unwind their positions, which will ultimately reverse or neutralize any price suppression effects of their attempted naked short sales. And this explains why naked short-selling for price suppression isn't realistic and why you'll see that based on long-term price charts for both gold and silver, their values follow cycles or patterns.

The main point of it all is this is that, despite the many conspiracy theories of price manipulation for gold and silver, proof of such is lacking. As for all financial assets whose values are market-driven, there are bull and bearish markets over the long-term. Bear markets - or when prices are falling - don't equate to price manipulation any more than bull markets - when prices are going up - do. It's all about market demand, cycles, and the ability to time our transactions well.

Chapter 2: Why Cryptocurrencies Work

Now that you've seen why compared to gold, fiat currencies aren't real money; it's time to turn our attention to cryptocurrencies as a solid alternative, why they are much closer to gold than money as we know it today is, and why they'd work better than fiat currencies.

Low Risk of Disruption

According to David John Grundy, the global blockchain head of one of the world's biggest banks, Danske Bank, the only way anyone can stop or shut blockchains down is by shutting down the Internet itself. And by now, I believe you know that is practically impossible. It's like saying somebody can keep the sun from shining or the wind from blowing.

Portability

Unlike fiat currencies, cryptocurrencies can be easily transferred from one account to another using online gadgets such as computers, tablets or even smartphones. With fiat currencies, you'll need to do so physically or through the same bank. Plus, you don't have to bring them with you physically because they're stored in the Internet. So you can go anywhere with a good Internet connection and bring your cryptocurrencies with you regardless of the amount!

Better Value Storage

You can only consider an asset as a good value storage if it's able to keep relatively unchanged levels of utility or satisfaction over time. Applying this to financial assets, it means having the ability to maintain purchasing power over time. A financial asset's ability to keep value can be estimated through what is called as fundamental analysis, which takes into consideration both the quantitative and qualitative aspects of such an asset.

The ability to keep or store value has become the primary foundation for investing or HODLing cryptocurrencies like Bitcoin, Ethereum, and others. But can cryptocurrencies be really relied on to store value and if they are, can they do it well?

The Gold Comparison

Don't be surprised to find cryptocurrencies being compared or likened to precious metals, i.e., Bitcoin to gold and Litecoin or Ether to silver when justifying cryptocurrencies' ability to store value over the long term. One of the reasons - albeit a shallow one - is the color of cryptocurrencies. Bitcoins are visually represented as color gold while Litecoins are visually represented as silver. But there are more than just visual cues that justify the belief in cryptocurrencies' ability to store values like the two most precious metals on Earth. We mustn't dismiss behavioral economics that underlie both asset classes. When more and more people start believing that cryptocurrencies like Bitcoin, Ether, or Litecoin are able to store value the way precious metals like gold and silver can, it can help push the prices of these cryptocurrencies upward. When their prices do go up over time, then it's highly possible that they'll be able to keep or maintain their values within a specific period of time.

Comparisons to precious metals, e.g., Bitcoins to gold, can be a very strong factor that can influence the perspective of general markets regarding Bitcoin's and altcoin's abilities to retain or store value in the long term. And this can have a huge impact in terms of the number of investors who'll view cryptocurrencies in general as good investment vehicles.

Limited Quantity, i.e., Deflationary

Just like gold in its physical form, cryptocurrencies like Bitcoin typically have a limited quantity of units, which is defined or set in their respective blockchain protocols. Bitcoin, for example, has a cap of only 21 million units that can ever be created. Litecoin on the other hand has an 84-million unit cap that's also controlled by its operating protocols. This is what makes cryptocurrencies deflationary or disinflationary over the long haul.

Remember our discussion earlier on supply and demand and how asset values are affected by changes in both? Because cryptocurrencies have a fixed number of units that will ever be minted, their supplies relative to the quantities of goods and services it can buy in the future is effectively shrinking. That means its purchasing power can be expected to increase over the long haul and can have deflationary effects on goods and services.

Independence from Other Asset Classes

Compared to all other financial asset classes such as stocks or fiat currencies whose values fluctuate depending on the pronouncements or moves made by central bankers or financial regulators, the real value of gold and silver can't be manipulated by any central monetary authority regardless of their macro-policy decisions. Because of its autonomy from any monetary authority, precious metals like gold and silver are able to withstand price shocks over time, which makes them very good storages of value in the long term.

Cryptocurrencies are like gold in that they're generally decentralized and autonomous by nature. This means just like gold, government decisions or policy changes have little direct impact, if at all, on their long-term values. The amount of decentralization and autonomy can be a hot discussion topic among cryptocurrency users and investors, where some favor the full autonomy version while others feel more comfortable with some compromise, i.e., hybrid combinations of some form of governance (not from the government) and decentralization. In general, cryptocurrency governance models can vary greatly with some adopting a balanced power structure among its users when it comes to major decision making on one end while others go for the benevolent dictatorship model on the other hand. And in between the two are various other combination or hybrid models. But generally speaking, cryptocurrencies with more decentralized systems may do a better risk in terms of hedging against the risk of their values being influenced or tampered with by regulators.

Underlying or Intrinsic Values

Assets that are considered to be true storages of value have underlying characteristics that serve as foundations for their values. In layman's terms, such assets have intrinsic utility values, i.e., practical uses that give them their values. Gold, for example, is used for manufacturing jewelry and electronic parts such as semi-conductors. Land or real estate's underlying value or utility is their capacity for having structures built upon them and the amount of foot traffic their areas get.

When it comes to underlying utility value, cryptocurrencies have a lot of potential. In particular, cryptocurrencies hold a huge promise in terms of changing the way financial transactions are done online, which include contracts enforcement, records keeping, and payments. As the use of cryptocurrencies like Bitcoin, Litecoin and Ether becomes accepted in more and more markets, their practical utility values increase even more, which can increase their values over the long haul.

Impossible To Fake

The blockchain technology is a revolutionary one in terms of facilitating online transactions and data or record keeping. Being such, it's practically impossible to produce counterfeit versions of it. And as blockchains continue to evolve, it becomes even more impossible - if such a term exists - to produce fake cryptocurrencies that can be used to buy stuff.

Impossible to Control

Particularly for cryptocurrencies whose market capitalizations are already in the billions of dollars such as Bitcoin and Ether, one would need a huge amount of money to transact enough units of such cryptocurrencies just to be able to influence or manipulate their prices. When you take a look at Bitcoin, for example, whose average market capitalization hovers somewhere around US$50 billion, one would need at least US$10 billion to play around just to be able to manipulate demand and supply. Even if you're talking about Ether, whose average market cap is much smaller at "only" around US$25 billion to US$30 billion, one would still need a couple of billion dollar worth of transactions just to sway prices to his or her favor.

The Little Guy Gets In More

Unlike stocks and other financial assets that require relatively high amounts of investment capital, cryptocurrencies have low barriers to entry. That means even people who only have relatively small amounts of money to invest can easily get in. As such, cryptocurrencies, in general, have a higher number of investors participating in them to the point that it becomes practically impossible to manipulate the market.

Relative Security

Lastly, cryptocurrencies are virtually impossible to rob if you do your homework of using the right kind of storage, which we'll talk about later. But if you just leave them in your cryptocurrency exchange account, that's the only time when it's at high risk of being hacked and stolen. So if you follow my advice later on regarding storage of your Bitcoins or other cryptocurrencies, you can make your cryptocurrencies so safe that they'll be practically impossible to steal.

Chapter 3: How to Store Your Bitcoins or Altcoins Safely

In Chapter 2, I mentioned that if you do your homework and follow my advice, your cryptocurrencies can be practically impossible to steal or hack. In this chapter, I'll spill the beans on how you can do that, which can be summarized in 3 words - a cryptocurrency wallet.

A cryptocurrency wallet is where you store your cryptocurrencies. This may be considered a cryptocurrency investing because the financial assets you're dealing with have no physical counterparts, i.e., they're digital. And because they're digital, you can only store them via a digital storage facility, i.e., a cryptocurrency wallet. The only question is what type of wallet will you use?

There are two general types of wallets: hot storage and cold storage. Hot storage wallets are those that are online or Internet based. Cold storage wallets, on the other hand, are those that are offline or aren't connected to the Internet. So which of the two is best for safely HODLing your cryptocurrencies? If the only way to steal or rob your cryptocurrencies is via hacking, then the obvious answer is cold storage or offline wallets, which come in two general variants: paper and hardware. And I suggest using both.

But before I explain how these two cold storage wallets work, allow me to explain how cryptocurrency storage, particularly the blockchains, works. When you buy cryptocurrencies from any particular exchange, your transaction is assigned a public key that is linked to the number of units of a cryptocurrency that you bought. Your cryptocurrency exchange, on the other hand, assigns private keys that corresponds to your public keys. Therefore, your private keys are your lifeline to your cryptocurrencies, and if you lose or forget them, you can say goodbye to your cryptocurrencies.

For others to successfully "steal" your cryptocurrencies, they must get hold of your private keys. It's like your ATM card's personal identification number, which will allow other people to withdraw from your account without your permission. When you leave your cryptocurrencies in your hot wallet, i.e., your cryptocurrency exchange account, you put them at risk of being hacked and stolen. That's why as soon as you're done buying your cryptocurrencies, you must transfer them, including your private keys, to your cold storage or offline wallet.

Ok, now that we've got that covered, I can explain how the paper and hardware wallets work. The paper wallet isn't really a wallet but more of a backup. Write your private keys on a piece of paper and put that paper in a place where it's virtually impossible to steal or destroy them. A very good place to do so is a fire-proof vault or safe. Another's a safety deposit box.

Hardware wallets are USB-type devices that you can store your cryptocurrencies and its private keys in. These are devices whose sole purpose is to hold your cryptocurrencies and as such, they're offline most of the time. To use them to receive or transfer your cryptocurrencies from and to your cryptocurrency exchange account for executing transactions, you only need to plug it into the USB port of your Internet-connected desktop or laptop computer and follow instructions.

Cold storage hardware wallets are much safer compared to software wallets, i.e., apps installed on gadgets for two reasons. One is if it's installed on a device that's mostly online, then the risk for getting hacked is still fairly high. Second, even if you install it on a device that you only connect to the Internet for transacting in cryptocurrencies, there's still a risk of loss if that computer is damaged beyond repair or even if it can still be repaired, the computer technician to whom you'll have it repaired can possibly hack the drive and consequently, your wallet. With a hardware cold storage wallet, the risk of losing your private keys due to hardware damage is much, much lower. Further, using a paper wallet as a backup can help mitigate such a risk. Some of the most popular hardware wallets include Trezor, KeepKey, and Ledger Nano. They may cost a bit, but they're worth the investment.

Chapter 4: Is Bitcoin dead?

Because of the rapid rise in value of Bitcoin, especially in December 2017 when its market price quadrupled in just a couple of weeks, and its subsequent price retreat in January 2018, many people were led to believe that Bitcoin's just an asset bubble that has already popped. In other words, they believe that Bitcoin's as good as dead.

But while the huge returns Bitcoin and other major cryptocurrencies have generated in a relatively short period of time is reminiscent of the Internet and Holland Tulip bubbles in the past, it's fundamentally different than those two assets. As such, Bitcoin and other noteworthy altcoins have a much brighter future compared to the two aforementioned assets.

The following are indicators that Bitcoin isn't dead yet and more importantly, it's going to be around for a long, long while.

More and More Legal

Not to say that Bitcoin's an illegal endeavor but what I'm saying is that it's becoming more and more accepted as legal tender. You see, one of the most serious challenges facing Bitcoin with regards to being accepted in the financial services mainstream is acceptance by government monetary authorities (lawmakers and regulators alike), which is hampered by its decentralized and autonomous nature. Governments hate what they can't control so Bitcoin's not exactly in their good graces - at least not yet. But recent developments in major economies indicate that government acceptance, in general, is becoming more and more likely.

Japan announced back in April 2017 that it would officially start treating Bitcoin as a valid or legal alternative payment method and as of 2018, it already is. This has made

Bitcoin practically part of the Japanese mainstream financial system as more and more merchants in the Land of the Rising Sun have officially started accepting Bitcoin payments.

Other major world economies like Russia and Australia have also released similar statements indicative of Bitcoin being accepted as a form of legal tender in their respective economies soon. As more and more major world economies accept Bitcoin as a legit payment method, the rest of the world is highly likely to follow suit.

More Stores

More than just government pronouncements, Bitcoin's acceptance among merchants continues to rise because of the confidence shown by some of the world's biggest companies in accepting payments using the granddaddy of all cryptocurrencies. These companies include Microsoft, Overstock, and Rakuten.

But more than just riding on the bandwagon of these big companies, there are fundamentally sound reasons for the rising number of merchant acceptance of Bitcoin. One of them is transaction fees, which are much less than what credit cards charge to its merchants. Other practical advantages Bitcoin as payment has are the ability to reach new customers from regions in the world that are not yet reached by mainstream banking institutions and elimination of chargeback fraud. With the expected rise in mainstream acceptance by merchants, demand for Bitcoin is expected to rise and of course, its price can be reasonably expected to rise over the long term as well.

Wealth Storage

Remember our discussion in a previous chapter concerning cryptocurrencies' ability to store value and its relationship with functional value? The increasing acceptance of Bitcoin in many of the world's financial markets, particularly in countries that are experiencing economic distress, gives the granddaddy of all cryptocurrencies increasing functional value. In such distressed economies as Bolivia and Venezuela, local currencies' values continue to deteriorate to the point of becoming worthless. In such economies, Bitcoin is becoming more and more accepted as a mode of payment, which means its functional or utilitarian value is increasing. So as their local currencies are becoming less and less valuable, Bitcoin is becoming more and more precious and as a result, is becoming an even better storage of value for citizens of such countries.

Walking Dead...No!

As you can see, Bitcoin's very much alive and kicking and based on the indicators I've just enumerated, you can expect it to continue staying alive. Bitcoin, being the granddaddy of all cryptocurrencies, has the highest market capitalization and best performance track record, both of which will continue to make Bitcoin more and more accepted in the international financial mainstream. And as that happens, the likelihood of Bitcoin dropping dead will become even more statistically impossible.

Chapter 5: Cryptocurrency Pre-Hodling Strategies

Before we discuss how to hodl in more detail, I want to make a distinction between two investment methods: the long-term approach and the short-term approach. The short-term approach is more popularly known as trading, i.e., buying and selling of financial assets within a relatively short turnaround time like within a few hours, or at most, a couple of weeks. The long-term approach, also known by the names buy-and-hold and buy-it-forget-it, is an approach where the investment time horizon is - you probably guessed it right - long. By long, I mean at least 1 year.

Hodling falls under the long-term, buy-and-hold approach. Hodling has its share of advantages over the short-term approach. One of them is time. With the short-term approach, you have to be on top of your positions most of the time so you can time your transactions well. This is especially true for financial assets whose prices are very volatile, like cryptocurrencies. With the long-term approach, the bulk of the work you'll need to do will be prior to buying your financial assets, i.e., research. After doing your homework, you buy the financial asset you believe is your best bet and forget about it. All you'll need to do is update yourself on the price of your investment once a week or even once a month. Because your investment view is long-term, you won't be affected by the price fluctuations in between and hence, only need minimal management or monitoring.

Another advantage is cost. In a perfect world, every transaction shouldn't cost a dime. But our world ain't perfect so you'll need to pay transactions fees for every financial investment transaction. With trading, you'll trade more often, which means more transactions fees. With a long-term approach, a.k.a. hodling, the number of transactions you'll have to make are few and far in between, which means less transactions fees.

Now that I've gotten the distinction out of the way let's jump into how to significantly increase your chances of hodling successfully. For better appreciation and understanding, I'll divide this topic into two main sections: Before and during hodling. We'll focus on before HODLing in this chapter.

Ask Yourself Why

Remember what I wrote earlier about how bulk of your hodling work will be in the beginning, i.e., prior to your actually hodling your cryptocurrency investments? Good. Now let's buckle down to work! The very first thing you'll need to do is know your reason for hodling.

When you examine the lives of people who have achieved so much in their lives, one common thread that runs through them is awareness of their life purpose. In other words, they know why they're doing what they're doing. And more importantly, I guarantee you that if you examine each of their reasons, you'll find those reasons to be very meaningful or compelling ones. Therefore, you'll need to have a compelling reason for hodling any financial asset, which in this case is cryptocurrencies.

Why is this crucial? Hodling successfully will require self-control and perseverance, especially during times that prices are down, i.e., bear markets. It is during such moments when your emotions can become so strong that they override all logic and make you do things you'll probably regret later on.

But while anybody's reason for hodling's very obvious, i.e., make money, it's not a very compelling one. In fact, it's a very generic and shallow one. I'm talking about a deep, compelling, and personal reason. To better help, you figure this out, ask yourself deeper questions such as why do you want to make money of this investment? Is it so you can have enough money for your child's college education 15 years from now? Is it so you can retire early? Or is it so you can travel around the world by the time you turn 60 years old? The more personal and bigger your reasons are, the more compelling they can be.

When you're tempted to switch to a riskier cryptocurrency that's been increasing in value at a faster rate than the relatively less risky but consistently performing cryptocurrency you're hodling, knowing that you're doing this to minimize the risk of your child not being able to go to college can help you exercise self-control and avoid taking excessive risks and gambling away your child's future. When you're tempted to unload your cryptocurrencies simply because they've dropped in value even though all indicators may point to a bright future ahead, knowing that you're doing this so you can retire early can help you resist the temptation knowing that unless you actually sell your cryptocurrencies at a loss, your market loss is just a theoretical one and can still be recovered.

Minimum Rate of Return

When you know how much your investments need to earn at the minimum, it'll be easier for you to choose your investments wisely. And by wisely, I mean choosing investments that are neither too safe but unprofitable nor potentially very profitable but also excessively risky. When you know how much return you need to accomplish your hodling goals, you put yourself in a good position to take on investments that will help you accomplish your goals for the least possible risk.

So how do you know you minimum rate of return? First thing you'll need to know is how much money you need to have by the end of a certain period, e.g., after 5, 10, or 15 years. Then, determine how much money you can afford to set aside for investing. Finally, determine the rate of return based on your expected future value (the amount you need to have in the future) and present value (your available funds for investing or hodling). And when you've determined that, make it your minimum expected rate of return and choose only those cryptocurrencies whose average annual rate of return is equal to or more than your minimum required.

Risk Appetite

This refers to how much loss you are willing to take in the event your investments turn sour. Why is this an important consideration? It's because there's no such thing as risk-free investments and the higher the expected returns on investments are, the higher the financial risks you must be willing to take. So there is a possibility that your investments won't be able to give you the returns you're after. And the worst thing that can happen is you lose money on your investments, which can be as much as all of it. By knowing how much you're able to comfortably lose, you'll be able to determine whether or not to invest in a specific financial asset such as cryptocurrencies. And if you decide you want to invest in a specific financial asset despite the risk, knowing your risk appetite or tolerance can help you determine how much money to invest.

When figuring out how much cryptocurrencies to hodl, there are two ways you can estimate your risk appetite. One way is to think about how much money you can comfortably lose. There are two benefits to this approach. The first is this: your finances won't be seriously affected if the worst case scenario happens. Investing your entire savings in cryptocurrencies is a foolish idea because if the price goes down by a significant amount, you might not have enough money for your personal needs when something unexpected happens like getting hospitalized or if you accidentally wreck your car. But if you invest an amount beyond what you really need to live a comfortable life, you can live with worst case investing or hodling scenarios.

The second benefit to this approach is you won't be pressured when prices of your cryptocurrencies go down or fluctuate wildly. When that happens, your emotions won't get the better of you and because you can be more objective when it comes to your cryptocurrency holdings, your chances of successfully riding out temporary investment "storms" are much higher.

The other way you can estimate your risk appetite is by determining an amount of money you strongly believe you won't need to use within the next 1 or 2 years and beyond. How's this a good basis for determining how much to invest in cryptocurrencies or other financial assets? Hodling is a long-term endeavor. As such, you need to be able to keep your investments intact so it can ride out temporary dips in prices if any. For you to be able to do this, you'll need to make sure that the money you're going to invest is an amount that has a high probability of not being needed in the near future.

Read the Damn White Papers

Especially if you plan to invest in an initial coin offering or an ICO, which is the cryptocurrency equivalent of initial public offerings or IPOs of stocks and bonds, you'll need to read the white papers of the cryptocurrencies you're interested to hodl. But what are white papers?

Before we get to that, we need to talk about ICOs first. An ICO is a way by which creators of a cryptocurrency raise enough funds to launch a new one. These fundraising activities are unregulated, considering the autonomous and decentralized nature of cryptocurrencies. Compared to the usual fundraising activities of mainstream investment banks and other financial institutions, ICOs are way less rigorous and regulated, which makes them easier to do.

ICOs worth their salt will always give out white papers, which is the ICO equivalent of an IPO's prospectus. A white paper is a document that elaborates on the details of the fundraising activity, i.e., ICO. These details include among others the purpose for the fundraising activity. As a prospective investor, it's crucial that you know as much as you can about the ICO you plan to get into so you can have a very solid idea of whether or not it's legitimate and whether or not it has very good investment potential. White papers are written by people from a wide range of backgrounds who are knowledgeable about the coin or token to be issued as well as the financing of such like lawyers, PR practitioners, experienced business men, and information technology experts, among others.

White papers are created and distributed to the investing public to give them a clear idea what the ICO is really about and in the process, foster a good level of trust from them. White papers - just like prospectuses - can help establish the legitimacy of an upcoming ICO and thus, is crucial for its success. And for you, as an investor, the white paper is the primary means by which you can learn all there is to learn about a soon-to-be-issued cryptocurrency. Through white papers, you can make the most informed decision possible about whether or not to invest in an ICO. So when you see an ICO already being sold without a white paper, that should be a red flag already concerning its legitimacy or if not, the quality of that ICO.

So what are the things a good white paper should contain? These include:
- The ICO's vision;
- The underlying technology for the token;
- The token or the project's unique selling proposition (USP), i.e., what current problems or challenges it can effectively address, why being able to effectively address such challenges is important, and the token's unique characteristics;
- How the token will be distributed among its ICO subscribers as well as among the team behind it;
- Timeline of activities that need to be completed for the ICO;
- Language and focus of the white paper; and
- The people behind the token's development and their credentials.

Details such as these are crucial for your hodling success because these are the things that can affect the long-term viability of the token in question.

Reading the white papers is very crucial for spotting a potential scam. Of all the details white papers contain, there are three that can give you a good indication of whether or not the ICOs they're backing up are legit. These are the vision, the people behind the ICO, and the language and focus of the paper.

The vision part of white papers gives you an idea if the people behind the ICOs believe that they'll be around for the long haul or for the short term only. Legit ICOs are in it for the long haul so if their vision is either short-term or is vague as to the timeline, better think twice.

The people behind ICOs should give you a very good idea of the quality of their quality and their chances of being able to successfully accomplish their vision. Conduct a background check on the people identified in the white papers as being part of the core team, particularly their accomplishments, credentials, and where available, any scandals or issues involving them. Because they are the people who are responsible for creating and managing the tokens up for sale in ICOs, they should be the single biggest factors to consider when weighing the chances of success for ICOs. Or whether or not they're legitimate.

Lastly, the way that white papers are written is another indicator of whether or not they're legit. In particular, pay close attention to the focus and language of the paper. What's the paper focusing on? Is it focusing on the benefits with very little or no discussion on risks? If this is the case, then chances are it's either a very low quality ICO or worse, it may be a scam. Scams tend to focus on the potential benefits, making them seem almost sure or guaranteed, in order to make you feel so good about them enough to be duped. Legitimate ICOs disclose relevant investment risks so their prospective investors can make the most informed decision possible.

What about the language? White papers that are written very poorly, i.e., using inappropriate language or terms can be indicative of a scam. For example, try watching the TV show Designated Survivor and one thing you'll probably notice is how realistic the show seems, which makes it a legit high quality program. And one of the reasons why you'll probably think that way is because they use terminologies that are actually used in the White House or in politics. In the same manner, legit white papers will use terms and sentences that you just know is consistent with the industry. White papers that appear to be written by amateurs is a red flag.

However, white papers that meet these three criterions isn't a guarantee of legitimacy and high quality, as it's possible for scammers to hire professionals to write very good white papers for them. But what it does is tell you that there's a very high probability that the ICOs such white papers back up are legitimate and of good quality. That's why it's also important to research information outside of white papers. That way, you can validate the information you'll obtain from them.

Chapter 6: Cryptocurrency Hodling Strategies

Now that you've done your pre-hodling homework, it's time to discuss hodling strategies that can help you achieve your investment goals.

Use the Minimum Expected Return to Choose Your Cryptocurrencies

After determining your minimum required rate of return, it's time to do a bit more research for hodling cryptocurrencies that have the highest chances for success. In particular, you must research on the average rates of return on your prospective cryptocurrencies, particularly if you plan to buy those that are already being publicly traded. Why? It's because tokens being sold through ICOs don't have past prices to compute average returns with.

For illustrative purposes, let's say that after doing your research, you find that the average annual returns on Bitcoin, Ethereum, and Litecoin were 30%, 20% and 25%, respectively. If your minimum required rate of return is 18%, which of the three would you choose? Chances are, you'd go for Bitcoin without batting an eyelash because it has the highest average annual return at 30%. I wouldn't say it's wrong but what I can say is that it's incomplete. Why?

When comparing actual returns to average returns, they're rarely the same. Actual returns aren't equal to the average, but they tend to be within the range of the computed average in most cases. This means that actual returns can be higher or lower than the computed average by up to a certain amount. To optimize your chances of being able to achieve your minimum required rate of return, you'll need to choose investments whose most conservative estimated or forecasted future returns equal or exceed your minimum. And for this, you'll need to compute for the standard deviation, which measures the volatility of returns or how far can you reasonably expect returns for a specific investment to be from the mean or average return computed. Allow me to illustrate this in a way that you can easily understand.

Let's say that the computed standard deviation for Bitcoin, Ethereum, and Litecoin were 15%, 3%, and 7%, respectively. What do these figures mean? It means that you can reasonably (not perfectly) expect the return for Bitcoin this year to range from 15% (30% -15%) to 45% (30% + 15%), where 15% is the lowest expected return for Bitcoin for next year. For Ethereum, the annual return for this year to range from 17% (20% - 3%) to 23% (20% + 3%) and for Litecoin from 18% (25% - 7%) to 32% (25% + 7%).

Now, compare the lowest expected returns for each of the three cryptocurrencies. Bitcoin's is 15%, Ethereum's is 17%, and Litecoin's is 18%. Given your minimum required rate of return, the wise choice would be Litecoin because its lowest expected annual return for this year is the only one that satisfies your 18% minimum requirement. Without the benefit of standard deviation, you could've gone for Bitcoin, which has a reasonable chance of registering a lower annual return than your required minimum. And even though its mean or average annual return's the highest, it's also the most volatile with the highest standard deviation, which resulted in the lowest among the low end of the expected return spectrums.

Diversify

A very crucial hodling strategy that you can apply to practically any financial investments, it means to spread your investment eggs in different baskets so that if one investment basket drops, your other investment eggs won't crack. And more than just investing in at least 2 cryptocurrencies, you must also make sure that you don't put all your investible funds in cryptocurrencies only. Why?

Because Bitcoin, Ether, Litecoin, and other altcoins belong to the same class of financial assets, which is cryptocurrency. There's a good chance that when something happens that concerns or can affect the whole cryptocurrency industry, the prices of all your cryptocurrencies may simultaneously take serious hits. For example, if the Federal Reserve makes a pronouncement that will make it more difficult to transfer funds from banks to cryptocurrency exchanges, it won't just be the price of your Bitcoin that will go down. But if you also diversify your investments to other financial assets, you reduce the potential impact of negative events on your total portfolio.

Cost Averaging

This is a very useful hodling strategy that can help you earn good returns despite substantial price drops in the cryptocurrencies in your portfolio. So how does cost-averaging work?

Cost averaging refers to a method of investing by which you buy more units of a financial asset (cryptocurrencies, bonds, stocks, etc.) when prices go down. You may be thinking: "Why the heck would I buy more units of a financial asset whose prices are going down?" That's a good question, one that I'm inclined to answer.

The principle behind cost averaging is this: by buying more units of a financial asset when its price goes down, you bring down your average initial cost per unit of that financial asset. So what's the significance of this? If your average cost goes down, your breakeven price for that financial asset goes down as well. That means you don't have to wait for the price of that financial asset to fully recover just to break even. And if the price eventually goes back to the same one at which you originally bought it, you won't just break-even but make a profit already!

Allow me to illustrate with a practical example. If you bought 1 Bitcoin at $10,000 and its price plunges to $6,000 afterwards, you would've suffered a $4,000 or 40% loss on your investment. For you to break-even, the price of Bitcoin has to fully recover back to $10,000. And for you to make a profit, you'll have to wait until Bitcoin goes above $10,000 per unit.

Now let's see what can happen if you employ the cost averaging strategy. Say you bought another unit of Bitcoin when its price dropped to $6,000. Now, you have 2 Bitcoins for a total investment of $16,000 ($10,000 + $6,000). By using simple averaging, your average cost of buying per unit of Bitcoin is $8,000 ($16,000 | 2 Bitcoins). Now, you only need to wait until the price of Bitcoin goes up to $8,000 to breakeven, compared to waiting for the price to go back up to $10,000 to break-even when you only owned 1 unit of Bitcoin. And when it goes back up to $10,000 per Bitcoin, you would've made a profit of $2,000 per Bitcoin or a total of $4,000 for your total investment. If you didn't cost average, you'd have to wait until the price of Bitcoin had gone up to $14,000 per Bitcoin just to register a $4,000 profit.

Conclusion

There's no denying that the next frontier in the evolution of the world's financial systems is Bitcoin and other major altcoins like Ethereum, Litecoin, Ripple and Monero. As such, good quality ICOs also have a bright future in the world of digital finance. But being able to successfully hodl and take advantage of the opportunities that cryptocurrencies - both existing and those that'll be issued in the future - require smart work and a whole lot of self-discipline. To the extent you can work smart and control yourself, especially your emotions is the extent you can successfully make money by HODLing Bitcoin and other cryptocurrencies.

To recap, HODLing refers to holding or keeping cryptocurrencies and that this word is a mistyped version of the word "hold" which has grown to be an accepted term in the cryptocurrency community. HODL is also a long-term approach to investing, which is can also be called as a buy-and-hold approach. To successfully HODL, there are two phases you need to get right: the pre-HODL phase and the actual HODLing phase.

The pre-HODL phase is when you prepare for taking positions in cryptocurrencies by knowing your investment goals or purposes, establishing your minimum acceptable rate of return, estimating the amount of risk you can take, and reading the damn white papers of ICOs, if you're looking to buy new tokens or coins. The actual HODLing phase involves choosing the optimal cryptocurrency based on the minimum expected range of returns, diversification, and cost averaging.

Thank you for buying this book. I hope that through it, I have helped you learn much about the art of HODLing. I wish you all the best in all your HODLing efforts and may you experience much success. Cheers!

www.ingramcontent.com/pod-product-compliance
Lightning Source LLC
Chambersburg PA
CBHW030038230526
45472CB00002B/565